Pitiful Poems

"And then, for a moment, all is still, and all is silent save the voice of the clock."
- The Masque of the Red Death, Edgar Allan Poe

The Looking Glass

His face was placed upon my wall,

the truth was insurmountable.

Behind the glass, his eyes did stare

through a mirror that was mountable.

Death, betrayal, hate and fear;

self-loathing in his presence.

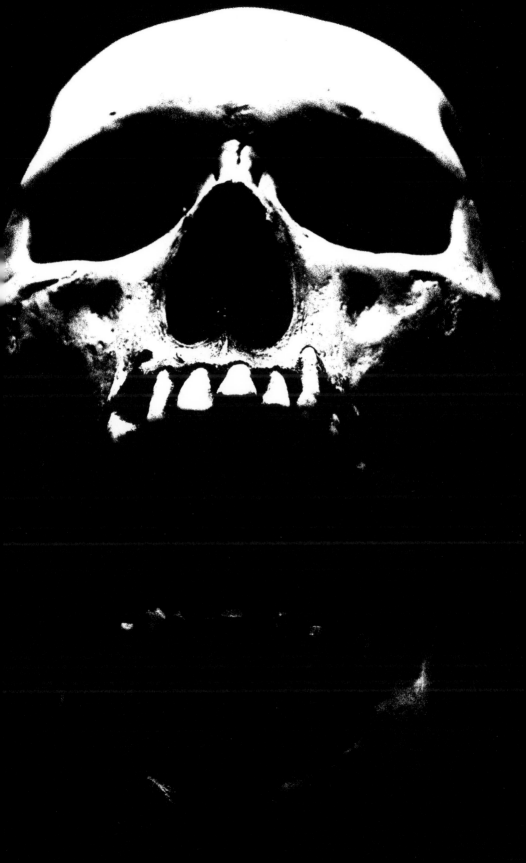

A ghastly way to spend your day...
in reflective iridescence.

The trap was set in vanity,

now penance doth await.

Bask in the insanity

no grooming can negate.

Pleasure can be found indeed,
in the walls of recreation,
and habits can be born
out of sexual frustration.

When one is idle, he falls prey
to the whispers of temptation.
A hand slips down into his pants...
commence with masturbation.

Now playing with your tackle
is as natural as cake,
but in this act of self-indulgence
lies a dangerous mistake.

His reasoning was boredom,
which sure enough sufficed,
then half way through this naughty cake,
he took another slice.

His hand came off, his mouth went down;
a surprisingly well-matched ratio.
The equation of contortion solved,
he had mastered auto-fellatio.

Every day, he sucked himself.
Every night, he had a taste.
He began to swallow his own seed,
recycling post-haste.

His appetite, for this strange act,
was cruel and un-receding,
but his appetite was not the only
thing that he was feeding.

From his sperm, a thing begat,
inside of him, unknown.
A thing that meant no longer
did he suck himself alone.

This evil creature spurred his hunger,
he blew himself red raw.
He did not think to hesitate
from fatigue or being sore.

He wasted away, a little more each day;
the only thing he ate was semen,
and even that was intercepted,
on account of the parasitic demon.

It *stole his pleasure.*

It *drained his fun.*

It *purely ran*

on *his own cum.*

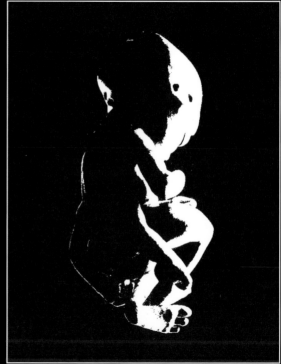

Bottle

I'm a bottle made of glass,
my neck is round and open.
If I should fall and shatter,
My body would be broken.

Each time it hurts. Each time I'm scarred.
A piece or two goes missing.
It might take time to fill the void.
Prepare to do some sifting.

My contents have been guzzled,
I've been thrown against the wall;
remorseless use of my good will
has aided my downfall.

Piecing together my remains,
my heart is left ice cold.
A fiery arrow penetrates,
with promises of gold.

This golden apple seems sublime,
but a bite I cannot take;
nourishment is but a dream,
a delusional mistake.

The factory that made me didn't have a fucking clue.

They fashioned me from misery and filled me with it too.

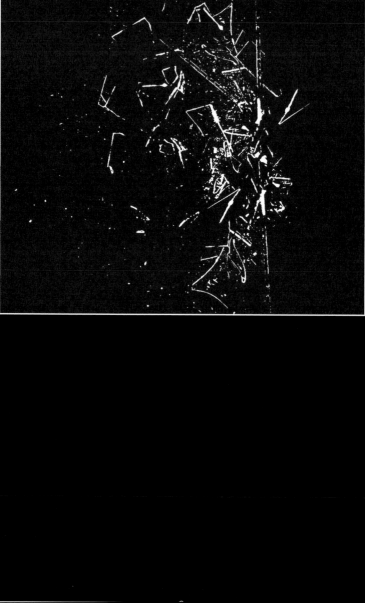

Harmful substances I did carry,
without a warning label.
Not sure if the ingredients
inside of me are stable.

Stitches

The Prince was waiting in his chambers,
for the Jester to come down.
His heart was thudding in his chest
and he throbbed beneath his crown.

Staring, glaring at the door,
patience not his virtue.
All he wanted was nothing more
than to smell his lover's perfume.

The Jester came at last,
though it had only been two minutes.
The Prince's red cheeks of pent up frustration
subsided once he was in it:

Their fragrant forest of love,
where no one else could clamber.
Desperately squeezing out all of the sap,
before it turned to amber.

Garments forgotten on the floor,
a blend of rags and riches.
A bond like this was surely more
than the boundaries of their stitches.

Away

Take me away, let's go on adventure.
It's really been too long.

Divine intervention, it's time for a rapture.
What possibly could go wrong?

Fly me away, I've been lost in dismay,
from here to Kingdom Come.

I've wilted and died a hundred times over.
The sunshine had all gone.

Drag me away from my hellish torment,
I'm sinking into despair.

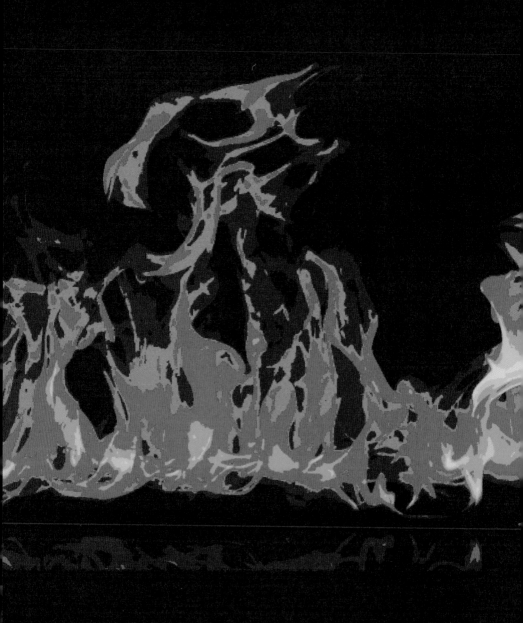

No more can I reach up to grab for a hand,
when no one's really there.

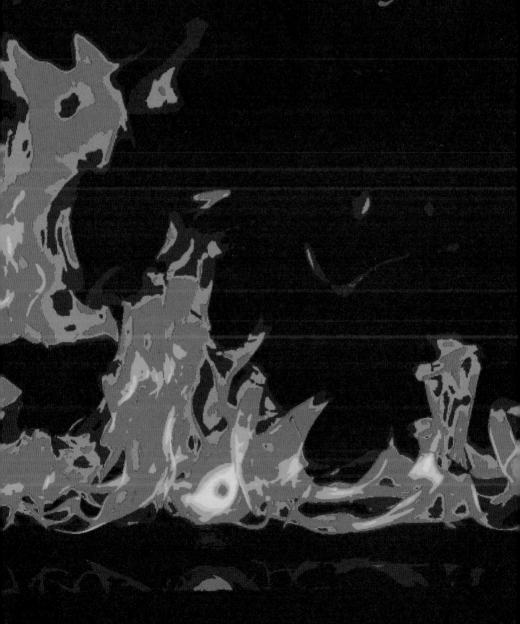

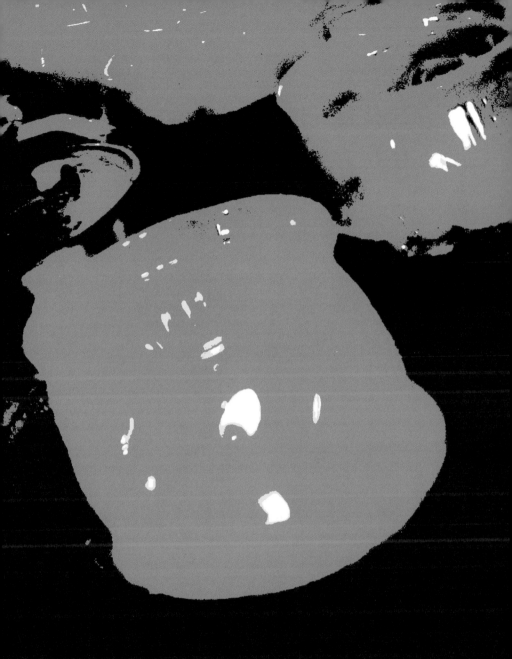

My pauper's hands might tarnish
your bejewelled and golden crown.

Put me out of my misery,
like many others would.

Crappy Shitmas

It's Christmas time,
there is a need to be afraid.
I've got presents to buy
and I haven't been paid.

My overdraft's maxed,
I'm over the limit.
This council tax
is too much, innit!

The dog has died,
he's still in his bed.
My kids are next too
if they don't get fed.

'Cuz times is 'ard,
I'm not having fun.
Is this really what
Christmas has become?

My wife had an epiphany,
so she packed up and left.
Santa gave her Tiffany
for a feel of her breast.

They ran off together
at my expense;
coal under the tree
to recompense.

At least I can use it
to burn myself warm,
and think about how
these harsh feelings were born.

Hatched, like a demon
from under a rock.
Melting, like candy
in a tarted up sock,

or "stockings",
as they're called right now.
They made foot-clothes
appealing, somehow.

Off to the high street,
it's rammed, like a goat.
Intimidated by the crowd,
I float

mindlessly through
the bright Christmas lights,
wondering what
I could possibly buy.

Indignantly contributing
to corporative riches,
whilst making myself poorer.
Those bitches!

Each happy face
I see makes me gag.
What can I say?
I'm a miserable slag.

I'm not in a nightclub,
but somehow, it's packed.
I'm greeted with an eye-full
of large Santa sacks.

I wish I could rip them
and split them and shout
"Crappy Shitmas you wankers!
Now get the fuck out!"

Fire

There's a fire in my heart.
It's constantly on simmer,
but then you come into my midst
and magnify this glimmer.

A wildfire cannot be tamed,
some may throw stuff in.
These embers are ephemeral,
as is their dreaded din.

Sparks fly here and there,
all so evanescent,
but the ones emitted from your ignition
are truly effervescent.

The flames unhinged, I burn out quickly,
the passion will desist,
and all is lost until I gather
the fuel I need to persist.

But energy is constant
and chemistry is clever.
A covalent bond has brought
our two atoms together.

Filthy Little Corpses

Two little dicky birds,
sitting on a stool.
One hopped off
and broke my fall.

Kill the little dicky bird,
kill it in the face.
Paul has taken
Peter's place.

Pretty Paulie dicky bird,
lapping up some wine;
alcohol numbs
his wee wings fine.

Choking on the nectar,
his eyes are wide ~ afraid.
Visions in his tiny mind
of his headstone being laid.

Poorly little dicky birds...
Life no longer dwells.
Fly away from mortal coils,
now they burn in hell.

Once effulgent, now repugnant,
filthy little corpses.
They'll drown you in debauchery,
then tie you up in torturey.

Laughing, laughing
all the time;
oh, how they love
a dirty rhyme.

Let them taint your stupid ears.

Let them peck away your fears.

Clever little dicky birds,
your soul is theirs to keep.
Haunt you in your daydreams
and swallow you in your sleep.

Tunnel

I saw the tunnel
and I knew where it led.
"Stop", a sign
at the entrance read.

Abandon hope
and the choice to turn back,
for all ye who enter
must stick to the track.

The darkness awaits,
but you're already there.
That's what you overlooked.

You stared at the blurb,
hesitating to read,
when you're halfway through the book.

This perpetual prism
of torture and torment
has a wicked end.

The light that guides you
gives you hope,
but it is not your friend.

For that light at the end of the tunnel,
leads to another tunnel.
The truth will be revealed.

A blanket of sadness.
An abyss of despair.
The evil will not yield.

Storm

I followed the path
that led to the sea;
portent of a fate
unbeknownst to me.

The sky clouded over,
but the waves remained calm.
A poor sitting duck's
always destined for harm.

Palm trees behind me,
sand under my feet.
Thunder clouds clash
as opposing fronts meet.

Bittersweet tension
resides in the air.
Heartache so faint,
you're not sure if it's there.

The Gloom in the Room

I remind myself calmly
that patience is a virtue.
Suffice to say, when left to die,
an eternity can hurt you.

Your time will come,
the pain will pay.
Cough up - I clench my fist.

A pauper's strife.
A straggler's life.
He holds on to his wish...

A taste of hope,
when all has died.
The truth to escape
the tongue that lies.

Bitter resentment
resides in his heart.
Insanity...
insidious from the very start.

Misery looms:
The gloom in the room.
The ominous gut-ache
of impending doom.

Emptiness dwells.
This is my hell.

Swine

There was a little piggy
who'd almost lost his way.
He'd wander 'round the sty for hours,
no friends with whom to play.

Then in came farmer Jack,
brandishing his fork.
Piggy squealed, because he knew
that Jack had a taste for pork.

Cowering in fear,
poor piggy reminisced...
A scar revealed the sore, sweet spot
the farmer's fork had kissed.

As Jack approached, the hog accepted
he had no place to hide.
The butcher smiled hungrily
as he primed the pig's backside.

As fingers disappeared,
both of them did whine.
At this point it was hard to tell
which one of them was swine.

Eyes were wide by candlelight;
a sordid sorry pit,
and fingers weren't the only thing
that vanished inside it.

This carnal violation
was sinful to say the least.
In this moment, Jack had truly
surrendered to the beast.

A final squeal, his eyes rolled back,
then piggy kicked him off.
He slumped with satisfaction,
but too close to the trough.

If you think he got off free,
you'd surely be mistaken.
He slipped onto his own pitchfork.

No one could have saved his bacon.

Siege

With every part of me that dies,
another part is born.
A soul so twisted, he recalls
the betrayal and scorn.

His eyes are heavy,
but he treads ever light.
He's weak,
but still strong enough to fight.

He has to...
He's been under attack!
A siege so unjust,
there's no going back.

The first blow got him in the chest.
Heart strings surely severed.
A charcoal hole to match his soul.
From love, he's left un-tethered.

A blow to the head, but not left for dead.
Recovery was promising...
A blow once more, then he was sure
the next one truly would kill him.

Alas, these hits were nothing more
than his own sweet bloody failures.
Time and again he would dust himself off,
ever searching for the right cures.

A hand gripped his throat.
Ah yes, he did choke.
That lump was there a while.

Worthless, begging,
pathetic and needy.
A man reduced to a child.

The final hit was one most deadly,
and one he won't forget.
Companions now, but really how
can this friend be truly kept?

This hit was quick
and surreptitious,
but above all,
most vicious.

He knows now, the error of his ways.
Never to seek out better days,
when all he has to hand
is not what he would plan.

Watch in patience.

Learn from malice.

Drink forever

from the vengeful Chalice.

Numb to daggers, only grazed.
Riding the wave, but barely phased.
Laughing in the face of evil.
Embracing his own insanity.

The call

Once upon a time,
the moon shone bright and full.
The hairs along my neck stood up
as I heard the lycanthrope call.

I felt it in my chest,
excitement running deep.
I had to look my best.
This was no time to sleep.

I ventured out, to see whereabouts
the pack partook communion.
They were hunters and so was I.
'Twould not be a delicate union.

The nearer I drew, the harder I chewed
on some imaginary meat.
I would make my offer to the pack;
an initiation to complete.

Finally, I stumbled on a clearing
where flesh turned into bone.
I could feel the humidity from their hunt,
their sharp teeth they did hone.

I ventured in the doggy den,
no need to be sagacious.
I tried to find my right mind while
alarmingly feeling salacious.

Blood is what they wanted.
The chalice laid in wait.
I'd need to spill my own before
a beast we would create.

Complicit, not contrite,
in carnivorous consecration.
Carnal carnage to consummate;
a lascivious, live libation!

Intertwined in ecstasy,
my fear had ebbed away.
Zoning out, I couldn't count
the wolves with whom I laid.

Succumbed to the one who bit me:
the pack's anointed druid.
Awed, because I now had claws
and was bathing in every fluid.

Eternal

As I walked along the path,
the people celebrated.
About to collect a gift,
my serenity dissipated.

Enclosed in a pen,
cooped up like a chicken.
Just another wayward soul
for the devil to stick his dick in.

I stopped and had a chat
with the master of temptation,
in amongst the happenings
of eternal congregation.

Sitting down,
as calm as a goat,
the truth was spilled
from his evil throat:

"You can never leave now,
you must party forever",
but was this really
a desirable endeavour?

He did not foretell
of my wicked lumber
and so, he released me
from my slumber,

to wake again
in this world so cruel,
in a shameful pool
of sweat and drool.

The Beast

He lurks in the shadows...
in the dungeon, he hides.
Where the dark rooms are warm
and the flesh goes inside.

He comes for you when
you have nothing to lose,
and regret has become
an acquaintance you choose.

He charms those around him,
with his cunning and guise.
One look and you've fallen
into his dark eyes.

An abyss of despair
awaits you in there,
but you will not know
'til you cease to care.

He'll penetrate harder,
when you want him to stop.
He'll show no remorse
and infect you on top.

...you'll let him.

Jinn

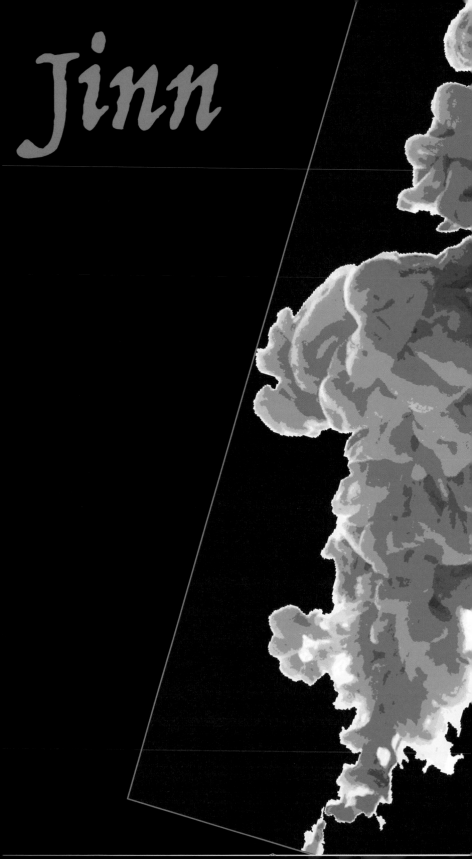

I can hear your whisper;
your solemn words of pain.

I know what you fear the most

and who you have betrayed.

I have always been there,

but you have never known.

I know, when you're by yourself,

you do not feel alone.

I *silently grant your wishes*

and give you what you want.

Always with a twist.

You're such a joy to taunt.

It's me that got your hopes up.

It is I who made them burn.

I'm the one who dusts you off.

You never seem to learn.

Cinnamon

It was night time in the jungle. The humidity of the air had relented slightly, but it was still warm. Everything was still. No creatures stirred and the only source of light was the soft amber moon, glimmering through the trees. On the floor of a small clearing, lay a pouch of cinnamon. Dropped. The fairy to whom it belonged was in the area. In her element, she danced into the clearing and swooped to reclaim her prized possession. With a smile on her face, she dipped into her pouch, taking a pinch of cinnamon, and sprinkled it over the nearest tree.

Suddenly the tree was illuminated in some sort of mystical light. All the plants around it breathed happily as she brought them to life. The fairy danced off to some other trees and carried on waking up the jungle. Then she noticed a creature resting upon a log. A man? Hesitantly, she crept up to him. He was perfectly still; not a breath escaped from his body.

A whimsical smile played across her face as she reached into her pouch once more and sprinkled him with her cinnamon. She then ran away and hid behind one of her tree friends.

The jungle man woke up. He glanced around and looked at his body, free from his paralytic slumber. As he rose, he knew someone had trespassed. The cinnamon fairy watched him, fascinated, as he made his mark upon Earth once more. He was bursting with life, and that was what she was all about. The jungle man could smell the fairy and he was angry. He hated cinnamon and her scent was all over his trees as they danced with the energy she had bestowed upon them. Infatuated with the dominant presence of the jungle man, the cinnamon fairy revealed herself. He froze. Such a bold move for... a woman?

They both knew, there and then, that the other was a creature of great power. Considering each other, they paced in a circle before hesitantly moving closer to investigate. Everything about the fairy was salacious. No one had ever enticed the man like this. She lasciviously licked her lips as they crossed bodies, and he felt a burning desire that had previously remained latent. The two forces of nature were locked in a tango, fitting together like a jigsaw, yet universally incompatible. The essence of each character rose to the surface as they danced, and the fairy soon realised that there was a reason for the jungle man's dormancy. Her aura was soft and bright, his was dark and cloudy. A clash that could never go unresolved. A brew that could never mix. Sparks flew as they whirled around each other with an intensity that caused hurricanes. They were both feasting on an unnatural indulgence; a forbidden fruit that was too succulent to throw to the worms. Like magnets they were stuck, the friction of the dance making more heat in the jungle than an Indian summer. Each time they collided there was a thunderstorm. The fairy knew she had to break away, but running was too risky. She stared seductively at him before moving in for one final thunderstorm, a distraction to mask her escape, but as she went to go, he grabbed her. She was instantly engulfed with his thick, black, smoky cloud and the life drained from her and everything around them. She dropped to the floor, dead. Her sweet scent drowned by the bitter odour of famine. The jungle man's eyes rested on the fairy. He never did like cinnamon.

About the Author

Craig Curtis Lee was born in 1991, in London. He's very dark and mysterious...
No one knows why he does what he does, he just does it.

To many he is wise, to some he is foolish.

Who even likes poetry anyway?

Printed in Poland
by Amazon Fulfillment
Poland Sp. z o.o., Wrocław

65943130R00054